# I AM

## A Poetic Ensemble

By Vitelle

Disclaimer: This book is presented to share the personal journey of the author. The author nor the publisher is offering or advising its content as replicable. The content is not intended to be a substitute for professional medical advice, diagnosis, or treatment, and does not constitute medical or other professional advice. Never disregard professional medical advice or delay in seeking assistance from a trained clinician. Neither the author nor the publisher shall be held liable or responsible to any person or entity with respect to any loss or incidental or consequential damages caused, or alleged to have been caused, directly or indirectly, by the information or the events contained herein.


Author Disclaimer: This book is in no way meant to shame or degrade any person or persons involved in my story. Names have been omitted for the privacy of others impacted along my journey. It is my sole purpose in telling my story that others may relate and as a result commit to improving their mental health, recovering from the damage caused by their own traumatic experience, and gain wisdom and encouragement to improve their own personal situation, whatever it may be. The crimes and offenses committed against me have not only been healed from but have also been forgiven. My story is only from my point of view and other points of view may vary. I can only tell my truth, and that is what I'm about to do.

# DEDICATION

*For Chelsey Rai Standberry*
*and her 3 little angels in heaven*

# CONTENTS

Preface – The Dash                          1

Introduction – Flag on the Field            4

The Skin I'm In                             12

Wisdom                                      14

The Horizon                                 16

Decisions in My Hands                       17

Last Night I Cried                          18

Unloved                                     19

Roaches                                     21

TV                                          22

Grandma's Porch                             23

Perspective                                 24

Distracted                                  25

Love Hate Relationship                      26

Released                                    28

Black Man on Top                            29

The Shape of the World                      30

Positivity                                  32

Teach Me                                    34

His Blue Shirt                              36

I Love You Too                              37

Every Movie End                             40

Falling from a Building on Fire             41

Aspirosity                                  43

The Never-ending Search for Me              44

Stop Playin'                          46

A Happy Home                          47

The Cop                               49

Bulletproof                           51

Prisoner of Age 18                    52

A Sudden Pause in my Soul             54

Ransom                                55

For a Moment                          57

Self Esteem                           58

Staring Down the Barrel of a Gun      60

Superwoman                            62

Dissolution of Marriage               65

Happiness Don't Last Long             67

Strangled Love                        69

For the Money                         72

Arraigned                             74

Her Heart is Darkness                 75

Alone                                 76

The Ugly Walls                        77

New Beginnings                        79

Who She Is Today                      82

I AM                                  83

NOTES & REFERENCES                    87

*I AM sent me.*

# ACKNOWLEDGMENTS

I thank God for all of life's experiences… good and bad.

For protection and guidance through it all, as well as the talent and ability to create such a masterpiece from much strife.

I survived so that I can testify, and I am grateful for the privilege.

For their roles in bringing this project to fruition, I am grateful to my beautiful friends, Natacha "Cha Cha" Martin & Dee Fox.

Special thanks to my photographer, Darwin Young, for the contribution of the brilliant cover photo that truly embodies the strength, power, and perseverance that this book represents.

…And to all of you, who continue to support and believe in me

… THANK YOU!

# Preface

## THE DASH

I've always known I was created for something great, and like so many others who can relate, I've had a tremendous number of setbacks, roadblocks, and distractions. This is the reason you are reading my very first published book more than twenty years after I first began to write.

I often feel as though I can't wrap up a story to publish it because it never seems to end. Take having been homeless for example: as soon as I think I'm almost finished with that particular book, I end up homeless again. There just never seems to be an appropriate moment to finalize and put a bow on it. So, I keep writing, waiting for "happily ever after" to happen, piling up the stories as life continues giving me plenty to write about.

I am wise enough to realize that a lot of the complications I've experienced were simply to keep me from finishing my books in the first place—any of them. This is a common trick of the enemy. If he can succeed in distracting you with all of life's painful experiences, then he wins. He wants nothing more than to keep you from writing that book; producing that movie or play; becoming who you were called to be—whatever that may be.

1

The only thing guaranteed for us all is birth and death; nothing in between is promised. Life is only what we make it. There are many of us who, not only recognize the need, but have an urgency to want to make our lives *worth it*. We want our lives to impact the people around us so greatly that all of the pain and suffering we've experienced throughout our lives will have been purposeful in the end.

A friend of mine said recently that every one of us has two dates on our tombstone: when we begin, and when we end. In between those numbers, all we have is that little dash…What will you do with your dash? When you look at it that way, you realize just how short that time is. Personally, I want my dash to mean something and not be as insignificant as…well…a dash.

Even as I struggle to write the introduction to this book, I'm reminded how important the gifts really are that have, up until now, been locked inside. I mean, I can barely finish a paragraph before I'm struck with severe heartburn; even stronger than the pain I experienced during childbirth. I can barely see past squinting through the unbearable headache, all the while, I'm fighting and saying to myself, "this book sure must be important"—and it happens this way literally every time I begin to write.

I'm no expert on good and evil, but common sense tells me the enemy wouldn't be trying so hard to stop me if it wasn't for good reason. Clearly, he knows something I don't.

So, I'm chuckling through the pain, utilizing birthing breathing techniques, and grunting between my teeth the resulting determination, "YOU'LL NEVER STOP ME!", as I continue with each keystroke. It's no surprise that I appear to be in labor as I birth this masterpiece.

I declare that, although Satan may try to stop me from doing God's work, he is already defeated! I can only imagine the Kingdom building results that will come of my following through with all the plans and ideas that infest my mind daily. I know they come from God with the intent to bring Him Glory. So, I will not give up; although I may have been stalled momentarily. I will keep pressing forward until my dying day, with the comfort of knowing I walked in my purpose and calling from God.

I encourage you to receive this same victory over your own life, and as you read through this book, don't just read for enjoyment or to be entertained. Each poem is from another chapter of my life. Each excerpt is a real experience. Later you'll be able to read in detail as each poem is broken down into its own book, and eventually movie. I'm speaking that vision into reality now, and if my testimonies can inspire and encourage you through whatever you might be going through, I can smile knowing that everything that was meant for my destruction, God turned around and used for good. With that knowledge, I can honestly say, "I would do it all over again". Victory belongs to The Most High, and I pray that He gets the Glory for everything He creates with my hands.

~

I also want to take a moment to remind you, before you proceed, that my fight is not with the people who played a role in my story. I do not call out any names, nor do I blame any person or persons involved. My focus is on the causes of the issues that myself and many others face, not the antagonists. I simply wish to be a part of the solution, not bring guilt or shame to anyone else. Besides, God will fight those battles for me.

Ephesians 6:12 says it best: *"For we are not fighting against flesh-and-blood enemies, but against evil rulers and authorities of the unseen world, against mighty powers in this dark world, and against evil spirits in the heavenly places."*

Remember that as you go through your journey and trails in life. Don't waste time focusing on insignificant factors. See the cause and seek God for the solution. As the word says, He will *"humble your enemies and make them a footstool under your feet"*. I rest in that truth.

# Introduction

## FLAG ON THE FIELD

You'll notice as you read through my collection of writings that follow, there is a similar pattern illustrating the multiple times in my life that I've reached the point of wanting to end it all. If you've never been suicidal, I don't expect you to understand. That's ok...I'm going to tell you about it anyway.

I've lost count of how many times I've clutched a bottle of pills, stood on the edge of a bridge, or held a razor to my wrists, thinking, "How do I know for sure this will kill me?"—more concerned with the awful thought of surviving as a vegetable than the fear of experiencing death itself.

I filmed a television series a few years ago called, *Flags on the Field*, by The People's Network. If you haven't watched it yet, I suggest you stop reading and go catch up on it now. It's available on Amazon Prime and on YouTube for your convenience. Should you choose to continue without binge-watching the entire series first, don't say I didn't warn you about the spoilers to follow.

The character I played was suicidal and I had to act out a very dramatic attempted suicide scene. No one on set knew how easy that would be for me... or how real. I did one take then instinctively went "back to one" as we do in film, prepared to do it again without coming out of the peak of emotion I had allowed myself to reach.

The director yelled out, "Perfect! That's perfect!", and proceeded to move on to the next scene.

I was confused and agitated because I know how important it is to have several takes just in case one has an issue, you look ridiculous, there's something in your teeth, or you said the wrong lines.—Which at this point, I couldn't even remember what I said but I was sure it wasn't perfect! I was still zoned out trying to balance the thin line between myself and my character, Shonda. Both directors insisted it was perfect just the way it was, so we moved on to the next scene against my better judgment.

In the next scene my character lies presumably dead on the floor. Her best friends Terry, Roberta, and Candace rush in after hearing a gunshot over the phone and assuming the obvious. The three friends find Shonda unconscious on her living room floor and began crying over their lost friend. Roberta, played by Chelsey Rai Standberry, lifted Shonda's head and hugged her tight against her chest, rocking forward and back, praying for her to be revived. Although I knew it was my character, Shonda, who they were expressing this concern for, I couldn't help but feel the real emotions and take them personally. It was at that moment I wondered, "do they really care about *me*?"

Would anyone be this distraught if *I really killed myself?*

~

Later on in the season, we see that Shonda survived her suicide attempt and has begun getting help for her problems. In a subsequent scene, Shonda gathers around with her girlfriends Terry, Roberta, and Candace again to tell them how much it meant to her that they were there for her and loved her during that difficult time in her life.

Of course, I knew my script, but one of the reasons I loved working with this director was that he trusted me to take the words to heart and let them come out in a way that's natural and real, rather than trying to speak every line from the script word for word.

Little did he know, these words really were what was on my heart at that juncture. I'll never forget this moment, as I poured out my heart to these beautiful women who I'd grown to love during this filming journey. I could never forget if I wanted to; it's on video. But until now, I was the only one who knew that it was Vitelle speaking those words, not Shonda.

Another one-and-done take. The tears poured out as I told my acting sisters how hearing them crying over me had saved my life. How I could feel their love and knew that they would never want anything to happen to me no matter what. I told them how I'd heard a voice from God while I was unconscious on the floor saying, "you still have work to do." I told them these things in front of the camera, as Shonda, because it was what the script said, (or close to it), but I meant them because it was what I felt and at that time, it gave me a reason to live. The women playing these roles had unknowingly kept me, Vitelle, alive.

~

It's these special moments while filming *Flags on the Field* that I reflect on as I mourn the loss of my dear film sister Chelsey Rai Standberry.

On September 20th, 2018 I received a phone call that Chelsey and her family may have been involved in a car accident. No one was really sure the extent of their involvement as they could not be reached, but we couldn't help but worry until we knew for sure what was going on.

I immediately got off the phone and began to pray that angels would be all around them and protect them wherever they were. Moments later my phone rang again, and I was informed that not only

Chelsey, but also her three young children were no longer with us. I was in complete shock. I fell to my knees immediately and yelled, **"God nooo!"** in disbelief.

It's hard enough to wrap your mind around the loss of a loved one. You expect that, eventually, your elderly family members will have to leave this earth. At some point in their old age, you attempt to come to grips with this inevitable outcome, not knowing when it will be but making an extra effort to enjoy each moment while it lasts. But to lose someone so young, so tragically and unexpectedly, not to mention so many at once…there are no words. My thoughts immediately went to Chelsey's husband, who had literally just lost *everything*. How could I possibly wrap my mind around that? How could anyone?

I was stricken with guilt as I lay on the floor crying my heart out, asking the same question I'm sure everyone who had heard the news was asking right now… **"why?"** The only difference is, my "why" was followed by, "it should have been me!". I was overwhelmed with guilt, as if I'd been driving the truck that plowed into them myself.

You see, just days before receiving this horrific news, I had begun planning my own demise once again. I'd had enough for the last time and the only reason I was still amongst the living was because I had my children to think about. So, I wanted to be smart about my impending suicide and make sure that they were well taken care of before I left this earth. I'd made plans to take out a life insurance policy, make sure their fathers had custody and would receive the funds, sold everything I had that was worth anything, and so on.

In fact, on the day I got that call, I had spent the majority of it selling my belongings. My objective was to stack up all the immediate funds I could gather in hopes to put something in their hands while they waited for the insurance to payout. It was only a matter of time before I completed the final step of this mission.

I had a few options in mind to ensure it looked like an accident, but I wanted to plan thoroughly so I wouldn't take a chance on surviving. The last thing I wanted was to be a vegetable, have a bunch of broken bones, or be paralyzed and still be here. I was extremely thorough with my planning—and yes, in case you are wondering, I had exhausted all my options and at this point, this plan *was* the most rational.

When people want to commit suicide the first thing other people who are not suicidal ask is, "what could be so bad that you would want to die?". Well, I can almost guarantee you that the answer to that question is always, "everything!"

Maybe it's just me, but I feel like in order for things to be so bad that I'd commit such a selfish act of leaving my kids behind and taking my own life, things have to **really** be piling up. Well, let me assure you, I've had a good 33 years for things to pile up and they were piled pretty high at that moment.

I've been cursed with this feeling of, "no one loves me" since before my birth. And rightfully so being that I was supposed to have been aborted. Growing up, I was never accepted by my own people, yet I was rejected by any other race of people I attempted to fit into. I've been an outcast my entire life and have spent it trying to please people, to make them love me, realizing consistently that I will never be able to please them all, and coming to my own constant conclusion that I am simply *unlovable,* and always will be.

"Unlovable" is naturally followed by its friend, "alone". Meaning, it doesn't matter whether or not I'm in a seemingly joyful relationship at the time, there is always so much that he can't understand about me, that I can't help but still feel alone.

Much of that comes from not wanting to be a burden on anyone else, as I feel I have been since the beginning of my life. So, when I'm facing my demons, as everyone does, I face mine alone and am reminded in those difficult moments that I have no one. No one cares. And that is my current reality…even if it's not.

When you combine all of these natural emotional instabilities rooted in me since my creation with all of life's regular issues I was experiencing: more bills than income, about to lose everything **again,** trying to figure out where we will live since the rent is going up in a month, physical pain I can't tend to because I can't afford insurance, working constantly to the point I forget to eat, can't sleep, still trying to make sure my kids are taken care of, pulled in every different direction, two different court cases, both a bunch of BS I won't get into…did I mention my teeth hurt, my back hurts, sciatica is real…I could go on…but I won't because somehow that phone call on September 20th made my mountain of problems look like an anthill.

Here I was, wanting to die because I felt as though I had too many problems to handle…but now, the Standberry family will never get to experience life's little problems again. I thought about Chelsey's husband who I'm sure would give anything for his kids to get on his nerves and pull him in every direction. I'm sure he would be grateful for another chance to hear his wife complain or gripe at him. If he'd only known.

Shame on me for wanting to outrun my problems so badly that I not only wanted to no longer live, but I longed for death like never before. So how is it that this family, so full of life, had theirs just ripped away?

Chelsey Rai was such a light in this dark world. I know people often say great things about someone after they die, but this is not one of those instances. Chels, as we called her, was truly an angel on earth.

I am positive that I never saw her *not* smiling. Unless of course, she was acting. She was a phenomenal actress who really put all of her emotion and passion into each character she played. I am truly blessed to not only have shared the screen with her, but also to have shared a true friendship. She was one of the first people I was able to let my guard down with.

After being hurt so many times by so many people, I couldn't even trust a friend to tell my secrets to without being sure they'd use them against me at some point for whatever reason. But I opened up to Chels, and she didn't disappoint me.

Like everyone else who loved her, I wish I would have called her more. I wish I wouldn't have missed so many events just because I live so far away from the city, or because I just had too much to do. Most of all I wish I could tell her, "thank you!"

As I lay crying on the floor, breaking for her husband, mother, and family—feeling guilty for considering my problems to be more than I could bear—the emotion that followed was an urgency to...LIVE.

All of these waves of emotion began to look very familiar; I was reminded of how Chelsey and my "Flag Sisters" had saved my life before. Here I was so sure, so adamant, about my suicide plan working to perfection. Everything changed when I got that call, and I vowed to never allow myself to go back into that dark place again.

Or at least if I ever felt that way again, I would think about how short life really is. I would picture Chelsey's smile and want to live, even if I couldn't do it for myself at the moment. I got up off that floor and changed all my plans because of her. Once again, Chelsey had saved my life. This time, I'd like to believe that she knows it.

The next day, I started compiling the book you now hold in your hands with a whole new perspective and determination to complete one of the many things I know I was put on this earth to do. That dash between my dates on my tombstone is too small. I have got to start making the most of that short time because the harsh reality in all this is, it can all be over in the blink of an eye.

~

Now that you know the "why" behind this book, I'll get into the what. As I mentioned before, I have several stories that I have yet to publish, but in my urgency to share them in a published format, I decided to gather together a collection of my poems, short stories, and journal entries written since I was a young girl. All true situations. All based on my reality at the time I wrote it.

I'll admit, the majority of the poems I've written over the years are not the most heartwarming. In fact, you may feel they have a negative tone or theme more often than not. Well, the reality is I haven't had the most pleasant of lives, and writing has always been something that's gotten me through the tough times. So, if you thought you were about to read a nice fairytale with a happy ending, you may want to go ahead and sit this one aside. It is not for the sensitive or faint of heart.

There were times I was able to encourage myself; other times, I just had to get the emotions out the best way I knew how. I hope that as you read—even the morbid pieces—you'll be able to relate to the experience or emotions and, if nothing else, realize you are not alone. So, in a way, all the writings contained in this book can be encouraging, depending on how you look at it.

I look at it this way…of all the things I've been through, the fact that you're reading this means I survived. At least long enough to publish my first book. My life won't be in vain if my testimony helps even one who hears it.

Of course, I'm hoping it will help many more than that. I have a hard time believing that such a troublesome chain of events throughout an entire lifetime could all be for nothing. Even amidst the many storms, I've consistently encouraged myself, "this has to be happening for a reason. I've got to be strong and get through this." I guess, if you're reading this, I succeeded. I pray this is the first of many successes to come.

You don't know.
You can't see.
You don't know what it's like to be me.

They say, "She's so lovely!"
"Beauty is she!"
But they don't realize that my skin is not what it should be.

I can see it in their eyes.
Exactly what is on their minds.
So, it comes as no surprise.
When they open up their mouths and the questions arise.

"Are you mixed?"
"Are you white?"
"What is your race?"

And although it makes me mad as hell,
I can't blame them 'cause they can't tell just by looking at my face

I AM BLACK!
I AM PROUD!
CAN'T YOU SEE?
ARE YOU BLIND?

In the way that I move.
The way that I speak.
And the way that I hold my head high.

No, I'm not conceited because my skin is light.
Do you have any idea how hard it is for me

'cause my skin ain't right?
And every day I hold all this pain within.
This is what it's like in this skin I'm in.

Look at this nappy ass hair!
So what that it's long. I've got Indian in there.
Quit smiling in my face, when I know that you don't care.
Every time I turn my back, you laugh.
And lie.
And stare.

Mom says it's jealousy.
But that ain't even fair to me.
Why should I have to suffer for the color my skin had to be.

Guess they wasn't lying when they said,
"Beauty's only skin deep".
If only others could see things the way I see.
I surround myself by the color that I'm supposed to be.
I don't hate them 'cause they're white.
They just keep reminding me.

So being misunderstood.
Not treating other's like I should.
I walk the path alone.
Unaccepted.
On my own.

And I hope and pray, that it ain't no sin.
But I just cannot accept this skin.

This skin that I'm in.

Everything I say is poetry
Every word I speak is rhyme
Words so deep, can't understand
Listen closely, may take time

See the way I walk, it's rhythm
See the way I move, it's mime
So, you better pay attention
'Cause I'm gonna blow ya mind

Every phrase, at least two meanings
May be taken different ways
Trust me, puns always intended
'Pends on how ya mind behaves

"'Pends, you say? That ain't no word!"
Listen, I make up my own
Take some slang, and throw some in
This is how I right my song

"Right, you say? You spelt it wrong!"
Purpose that's on what I did it
"What?", you say… You still don't get it?

Everything I say, I mean it
Everything I mean, I say
See no point in keeping secrets
All comes to the light one day

I cannot be a hypocrite
Because I only speak the truth
Even if it hurts sometimes
Chapter 1, Verse 20 book of Ruth

Used to read the dictionary
Now I'm studying the word

Seeing things, I've never seen
Hearing things I've never heard

Used to learn 'most every day
Now I'm learning by the minute
Changing all my wicked ways
Can't do it, if God ain't in it

Even though I've had it rough
God knows all the tears I've cried
Slow to murmur or complain
Some things must be kept inside

Training grounds, my life has been
Each circumstance that I've been in
Has made me who I am today
So really, what more can I say

So, as you read the words herein
A glimpse of where my life has been
Before you give the third degree
Don't judge by only what you see

# THE HORIZON

As I look out over the vast lands
Far off into the distance
At the place where the sky
meets the mountaintops
I think about the things I've been through
How far I've come
And how much
I have yet to see

I can't imagine how big the ocean must be
Or how high the sky from a plane
I can't imagine how far away the ground
must look
from way up there
Just the view sitting on the edge of this cliff
looking down
is inviting enough

I saw this distance once before
But I've come much too far
to give up now

How many blades of grass
are down there?
How many branches
on that tree?
How many flutters has
a hummingbird's wings?
How many buzzes
has the bee?

I've come much to far to jump down from here
Besides I've still so much to learn
I've still so much to see

# DECISIONS IN MY HANDS

I've got the pills in my hands; I could take them as prescribed
Or I can take them all, and hope for eternal rest
I've got the phone in
my hands, I could
continue to talk to
the stranger on the
other end, Or I could
run away to the
unknown where he is

I've got the hammer
in my hands I could
continue to hammer this
nail into the wall, Or I
could use it to reenact
the massacre in my mind

I've got the book
in my hands
I could continue to
read and believe, Or I
could stop, this happily
ever after isn't mine

So many decisions
I have yet to make
So many
decisions
in
my
h
a
n
d
s

Last night I cried for so long
I almost forgot why
The tension built and got so strong
I felt like I would die

I called to Him with all my might
I cried out loud to God
Eventually I saw the light
Though my mind was still a fog

I asked him why I had to stay
It's so hard in this world
He said "you'll be with me someday
Just hold on baby girl"

Then I felt him hug me tight
And wipe away my tears
He gently kissed my head goodnight
And then I had no fears

# UNLOVED

It's an emotion
        not included, or considered a form of depression
        but I'm telling you it is
I know because I've experienced it my entire life
        since I was a little kid

It started off as wonder
        I wonder why everyone hates me for no reason
        I wonder what I did

I soon realized that being born was my first mistake
        regularly reminded that she really wanted
            to end my life before it started
        I'm told I should have been aborted

Born into a family that I didn't resemble
        most of the time I forgot I needed to blend in
But I stood out
        like a sore thumb
A chameleon of personalities
        but I couldn't change my skin

I studied what made them happy
        made them laugh and love me good
A temporary solution
        I knew they never did
        I knew they never could

So, I learned to hate what the mirror reflected
        never accepted
            always rejected

One minute I'm the lightest, in the dark
        next the darkest, in the light
"What are you?", was always the question

No matter where home was for now
        I was always reminded
        that my skin wasn't right

As if my miscalculated casing wasn't enough
      I was also gifted with emotions
      then told I had too much

"Did you take your medicine today", was what she would ask
      if my laugh was too happy
      or my cry was too sad

So I learned not to feel
      or at least to pretend
Still unable to change the outside
      I mastered holding things within

Conceal… don't feel… put on a show…

I could put it in a movie
      and they still would never know

The amount of trauma
      the extent of pain
I carried into my adulthood
      along with the blame

At the first sign of rejection
      to my human responsiveness
I'm consumed with the reminder
      that feelings are bad

It's forbidden…
      what's wrong with you…
          there you go again…

I retreat into my closet of self-loathing
      trained for three decades to hate myself
      from the outside in

I'm told I'm supposed to love myself
      But how?
          No one else ever did.

Sitting here, time on my hands, I make this observation.
Humans are just like roaches.
They get on my nerves.  They
eat your food and leave
germs on
everything
they
touch.
The only
difference;
It is completely legal
for me to crush a roach.
Hunting them down and
poisoning their entire family is
completely civilized and justified.
I think I'm going to look into becoming an exterminator.

# TV

I despise that colorful box
the one that sends out moving
images, sounds, messages transmitted by
radio waves that gradually destroy our minds.

That idiot tube gets all the attention.
When people look at that pathetic screen,
they can't even hear or see me at all.
I sit there and watch them deteriorate
before the box that flashes a
florescent glow across their faces.
Watch them smile in ways I couldn't make them.
Hear them laugh, genuinely;
I've heard the fake ones.

I'm changing as the years go on
and so are the moving pictures.
It's no longer my baby-sitter,
it's now the mistress that my mister
abandons me for.
It receives all the time wishfully
reserved for me
and has, since its creation.
So, who am I, to think I am
when I have a replacement?

If you can't beat 'em, join 'em
I've heard since I was young.
So, I decided long ago
to put myself on one

# GRANDMA'S PORCH

I write much better outside.

The ideas flow through the wind that blows without ceasing,
     and the birds that exchange hidden messages
     through their never-ending song.

It's so peaceful here.
     That is except for the rambunctious children
     and the hardworking lawn mowers I can hear at a distance.

It's beginning to rain now
     and soon the streets will empty of passersby.

But that doesn't stop someone's grandpa
     from riding his Harley,
     breeze blowing over his empty scalp.

Neither does it stop my pencil
     from jotting down each thought, I conceive
     nor my mind from conjuring up incredible ideas as I dream.

Ah, the company of the outdoors.

As the battle rages on inside
     you can always go out
     to ease your troubled mind.

# PERSPECTIVE

In my world I see things
That no one else can see
I do not see the circumstance
I see what's meant to be

I see the evil lurking
On every single face
I see the visions of the past
Which, cannot be erased

I hear the sound of angel's wings
When someone has gone home
I even hear the silence scream
Whenever I'm alone

I always ask the questions
Most are afraid to ask
I see the person hiding
Behind the porcelain mask

I guess it's 'cause I've been through
Almost every situation
So when life gives me lemons
I see no limitations

# DISTRACTED

He was focused on his game
I was focused on his aim

Deeply focused
Wasn't focused
  on what I was sposed to be

My job was cleaning off the windows
I was clearing off the glass
But looking through it, you could see
I was more focused on his abs

Steadily focused
Wasn't focused
  on what I was sposed to be

He was sweatin' like a mug
Out there looking like a drug
Like he knew what he was doin'
Yeah, this boy was takin me through it

I need to fucos
Still not focused
  on what I'm sposed to be

# LOVE HATE RELATIONSHIP

It's like I don't wanna be his friend
    If he don't wanna be my man
It's like I don't want him in my life
    If he won't let me be his wife
It's like I don't want him hanging around
    If he don't really wanna be down

And although I'm sounding selfish 'cause I'm saying it
He's the one who's selfish
'cause to him it's all a game
And he's the one who's playin' it

I'm just tryna keep it real
Tryna tell him how I feel
He's always talking 'bout how much he cares
But actions speak louder than words

He don't care about me
He only cares about himself
Making excuses for his actions
When it's really something else

He's so predictable sometimes
He never says it,
but I, almost always,
know what's on his mind
I turned to him for love
But he was never there

It's like I wanna be his friend
    Without seeing him as my man
It's like I want him in my life
    Without thinking of ever becoming his wife
It's like I always want him around
    Without wondering if he ever
Maybe one day gonna be down

And I'm so afraid to move on
Because what if he changes his mind?
What if he comes around?

What if he's one of those guys who
when someone else starts to love you
they realize they always did?

And the funny thing is
        I know that he is

It's like I just want him to go away
        But my heart keeps wanting him to stay

It's like a love hate relationship, that I can't even explain.

# RELEASED

*Dedicated to my Uncle Dwayne McLemore*

Released, I'm a brand new me
Released into prison
Yet I feel so free

The ride home was a long one
So much was on my mind, so much to think about
So many emotions, bout forgot what it was like to be out

So much has changed, since last I was around
As much in me, as within my hometown
Released from the chains that had me bound

Jailhouse religion, don't believe in it
Don't matter where you get it
As long as you stick with it

Released, I'm a brand-new man
Set some goals when I was locked up
So that when I got out
I'd have a brand-new plan

And although so much has changed
Still so much remains the same

But me, I've honestly been rehabilitated
As the world around me faded
I just sat there every day and waited
For the day I'd be released

Released, I'm a brand new me
Released into prison
Yet I feel so free

Tell me sir
Was it hard
For you to get
To where you are

Did you have to bleed and sweat
Did you have to travel far

Did you start from the bottom
Slaving day and night

What'd it take for you to have the right
to eat your breakfast with the whites

And does it hurt
Does it still
Do you still know
How we feel

Are you aware
that they still stare
It's just behind your back

They still call you names
They still criticize
It's just because you're black

# THE SHAPE OF THE WORLD

How is it that someone can do so much good,
       but the bad things are all that ever show?
How is it that one can make so few mistakes,
       but soon as they make one, everyone know?

Why is it that all your enemies stay,
       but when you love someone they gotta go?
And why has it become so hard to tell
       who's a friend and who's a foe?

Why must my heart continue to feel
       such misery pain and woe?
Why do we keep on suffering
       for what happened so long ago?

And why does happiness not last long,
       but hard times go by so slow?
Why do we even have to go through
       hard times in order to grow?

Should I give up my dreams
       of being on tv, magazines and radio?
Should I just stop dreaming
       because the world is telling me no?

Why can't we all be honest,
       speaking wisdom and real with our flow?
And why is it only skinny chicks
       land the role in the video?

Why, when she's friends with all the guys,
       the first thing they call hers a hoe?
Why can't women uplift one another,
       instead, they make the other feel low?

If men have dogged her all her life
       should she give up finding Romeo?
Or should she believe, despite to signs,
       she'll one day be struck by cupid's bow

The questions could go on forever
       There's still so much I want to know

This mysterious circle of life will continue.

A circle. An object with mass
       whose matter travels to-and-fro

But the shape of the word is not round
       The shape of the world is… O.
       Oh!

I love the way he talks to me
I love the way he speaks
I love the way he fills me with
His positivity

He called me on the phone
He asked how, "How was your day?"
I had a really bad one, so
I had a lot to say

I had to walk 1000 miles
Out in the pouring rain
It was freezing cold, and now
My body aches and I'm in pain

On top of that all my teeth hurt
The dentist used a drill
I feel my head, it's getting warm
"Oh God I'm getting ill"

My mom's still trippin
My puppy ran away
I'm sorry to be negative
I've had an awful day

"Hold on", he says
"I'll call you back"
I just think,
"Yeah… Ok."

Alone with negativity
It started irritating me
So, I decided while I wait
I'd pray before it got too late

He called me back
With perfect timing
But this time
He did all the talking

I was so tired anyway
I didn't have much more to say

It seemed as though his every word
Answered the prayers that I'd been praying
I couldn't speak, I was in shock
Just listening to what he was saying

He spoke, not just to my heart
He spoke my heart to me
He replaced all my problems
With his positivity

Now I'm sure
I've found the one
I really am convinced
He took away my misery
Erased my negativity
He changed the way that I see me
And I've been smiling since

I know your hearts been broken
And I know it's hard to heal
But I want to tell you something
That I know just how you feel

You see my hearts been broken
So many times before
That I decided long ago
That I would love no more

So, when you came into my life
I tried to drive you away
I knew that if I fell in love
The price I'd have to pay

I was so cruel and hurtful
Thinking of me, and not of you
That I didn't even realize
You were heartbroken too

I struggled day by day
Trying to be the biggest brat
Trying so hard not to smile
When you looked at me like that

I guess we spent way too much time
You were so patient and so kind
Despite the fact I did you wrong
You stayed around, you played along

While I was driving you away
I really wanted you to stay
Forgot what I was fighting for
And now, I want you even more

You ask me what I want from you
I want your love and comfort too
I want someone who really cares
With whom, all secrets I can share

If I had known before
That you would never trust again
I would have never opened up
I wouldn't have let you in

But I'm glad I didn't know before
Or it may have been too late
And I would've never gotten the chance
To set the record straight

I realize we have a conflict
So, I've come up with a plan
And if it works out the way I hope
I can still make you my man

First, in order for this thing to work
We must make a compromise
I'll tell you all the truths
If you tell me no lies

We both have been heartbroken
Like the wings snatched from a dove
But I'll teach you how to trust again
If you teach me how to love

# HIS BLUE SHIRT

If it weren't for the sound of his heart beating in my ear...
I probably wouldn't have even believed, he was really there.

If it weren't for his skin, I could so clearly feel...
I probably wouldn't have even believed, he was real.

I haven't put down his shirt since he left out the door...
I'm afraid if I do, he won't be real anymore.

If I wake up in the morning and his shirt isn't there...
with his scent, and the color of blue...

I'll probably believe it was all just a dream...
that was much too good to be true.

At first, I just didn't wanna scare you away.
Then again, I wasn't sure if you'd even believe
what it is, I had to say.

I mean, it hasn't been that long…
How could I already be feeling this way?

And I don't want you to feel obligated
to give what you receive…
I want you to speak on your own free will
so that, I'll truly believe.

But I made a promise to myself
that I'd let you say it first…
As hard as it is to bite my tongue,
I know that if I don't,
I'll make things worse.

It's getting hard to catch myself…
Especially when I'm saying goodbye.
I try to look into your eyes and search
to see, if you wanna say it too.

My heart speeds up…
my stomach drops…
the tears begin to swell…
'cause I can tell, that deep
down inside, you do.

This is hard…
there's so much I must wait to do.

I keep dropping hints and clues,
but can't be too obvious…
'cause then, it'd be like
I told you to.

And it's funny sometimes, 'cause I wonder, since we're so
much alike
      If you're thinking, the way I'm thinking
          'cause if you are
               ain't nobody gonna be saying
                   nothing no time soon.

But maybe this is God's way of teaching me patience too.
      Perhaps this is God perfecting me,
          and preparing me for you.

So that I can say with my mouth,
      what it is I hold within
          So that I can know without a doubt,
               I'm not messing up again.

'cause I tend to love too much,
      too hard…
          too soon…
               then get let down.

So now I hesitate to love
      'cause I got so used to the sound
          of my heart crashing to the ground

And I know you keep telling me
      I shouldn't dwell
          on what happened
               in the past.  But it's the only
                   thing preventing me from
                      maybe saying it
                         much too fast.

'cause I wanna know…
      that I know…
          that I know…
               that I know…
                   this time it is gonna last.

'cause there's a thin line between love and hate
and I don't wanna say it too early
but I don't wanna say it too late.

So, I continue to wait…

See, because, we can mistake our love for lust,
as soon as mistake our lust for love…
and it makes it hard to trust
ourselves or anyone else.


'cause the word gets tossed around so much
like nobody listens any longer to what they say
but I don't want our love to be that
way.

The timing must be perfect…
We must be eye to eye
and face to face.

I know, God knows the time…
the place…
but me…
I have to wait.

I'm writing, in the moment, with faith that I can say,
by the time I read this to you…

The wait is finally over
and my dream has come true…

My heart, it knew I had to wait…
That's why this poem has no name

I had to wait, till I was through…
To tell you that…

## "I LOVE YOU TOO"

I stood there in tears, with one hand on the knob
    and the other on the door.
As I peered out into the night, I knew in my heart
    he would change his mind and come back.

So, like an *every movie woman* I stood there
    and waited for him to return.
I had every bit of faith, that soon, I would feel his kiss again.

Not later, not next week, but right then…
    As I stood there waiting for that *every movie end.*

Like *Pretty Woman*—she thought it was over, he was gone…
    It's what you least expect, when you least expect it.

The reality was, that he may not return…
    I just couldn't accept it.

Even as I walked away, I was sure I'd hear a knock on the door
    and go running back into his arms…
        reassured that he wouldn't leave anymore.

But reality no longer has me bitter at the *every movie conclusion,*
    'cause I know I'll get mine soon.

I know he'll be back, and we'll live happily ever after
    like *every movie characters* are sure to.

Once a damsel in distress… A princess in a mess…
    I found Prince Charming, and he brings out my best.

Somehow, he's caused this enthusiasm that I never knew…

Instead of worrying, he'll never return, I know that he will…

    'Cause *every movie heroes* always do.

# FALLING FROM A BUILDING ON FIRE

There are some things you can taste
And spit out if it tastes bad
There's no fear of what it might do to you
And the after taste doesn't last long

No one gets hurt
No hearts broken
And the only lesson learned
        is what not to eat again
Unfortunately,
        this only applies to food

I wish there were some way
to go soaring from a building
and never hit the ground
To see what it's like to fly
for just a moment
To feel that rush
and live to tell about it

I guess someone else thought this too
        Now, we have bungee cords and parasailing
        and such...

What is it about that rush of freefalling
        knowing you won't hit the ground?

I wish there were some way
to burn with fire
and never burn your skin
You could stop, drop, and roll
just to see if it really works
You could run into
burning buildings, saving lives

I guess someone else thought this too
  Now, we have fire suits and fireproof gels
    and such…

What is it about that rush of being set aflame
    knowing you won't burn?

I wish there was some way to kiss
without ever falling in love
To feel the touch of someone who cares
without starting to care yourself

What is it about the spark, those butterflies?
    It's even more satisfying than
    falling from a building on fire

I crave that passion.

Has anyone else thought of this?

Where is the solution?

Why can't I experience this
    without suffering the consequence?

# ASPIROSITY

To all my young aspirers, aspiring to be,
I keep inspiring the aspirers, as they inspire me
It's like one big circle of aspirosity

People keep trying to break us down
Shatter all our dreams
But as long as we keep aspiring
The outcome they want, cannot be

As long as we continue to shoot for the sun,
          we will land amongst the stars.

Either way, as long as we never give up,
          we may not make a trillion,
          but we'll make a million bucks

When I begin to doubt, I think of Martin Luther King
He had a dream, they didn't believe...
          He proved it to them, somehow.

And how much greater was his dream then,
          than our dreams now?

We are now, because we will be.

When we believe that it's already done,
          that's when, we'll see

# THE NEVER-ENDING SEARCH FOR ME

Constantly I've tried ways to find out who I really am
Writing songs, poems, even stories to discover myself
To sort out all these thoughts, that go on in my head

Writing what I think
Writing what I feel
Expressing myself in so many ways
It almost seems unreal

I realize my unique personality
But it's still so hard to find
Exactly who I am inside
Like, deep down in my mind

My mind controls what happens in me
Or so it has been said
But how much of an impact
Does the mind really have on who I am?

Does the mind decide who I am?
Or do I decide for my mind?
If I discover my mind, will I discover myself?
Or is it the other way around?

When we dream, the mind stays awake
And carries on without us
Seems strange to say, my mind is smarter than me
But it's true—you could say, it has a mind of its own

It keeps this secret from me
No matter how hard I try,
I can never trick it into giving it away
I can't find myself in there at all

I keep searching for myself,
Knowing all along that only God knows

Who I am, where I am,
Even what I will become

The never-ending search for me will always be…

Neva call someone a bastard
'cause they may not got a daddy

Neva call someone a whore
'cause they may have been there already

Basically, you need to know someone
       Before you crack a joke

'Cause you neva know when that someone's
       gonna slit ya throat

# A HAPPY HOME

I smell the memory, of breakfast being prepared
The sound of bacon sizzling, music playing
The sunlight from the open door, and cool Summer breeze
Both kiss my skin as I enter the room

She greets me with a smile, while singing hymns
With childlike excitement, I respond
Hungry for attention… eager to eat
My two little sisters giggle, happy as can be

Today is going to be a great day.

With much anticipation
I absorb the memories
The smiles on their faces
The way it's meant to be

I know it won't last long
I've learned to enjoy it while it lasts
Like every memory,
Even the good ones end up in the past

My taste buds remember the delicacies
That came on rare occasions
My heart quickly forgets the torment
Of yesterday's abrasions

I wish it could always be like this
I love my mother dearly
The joy she has today, that's never here to stay
If only the acts of today, were acted out sincerely

They come and go like Seasons
And with them, each time, take some of her away
They have their different reasons
It's all become cliché

Each time, I hate them even more
But still, can't help but imagine
That every day could be this way
A childhood I could fathom

She loves me, She loves me not
The petals fall to the ground
I know she'll always love me
When she has a man around

I choose to set neglect aside
In the moment, intentionally pretend
I know it never was for me
It always was for them

# THE COP

Mr. policeman look at me
Tell me what it is you see
Sir, can you not hear my plea?
Can you not tell, I'm trying to flee?

Why can't you tell, that all's not well?
It's not all as it seems
Why can't you look into my eyes,
And hear my silent screams?

I thought you were a hero
But now, I see you're not
Where were you at the other day
When I was almost shot?

Or then, when I was beaten and raped
And put out on display
It's almost like you looked at me
And simply walked away

And they call you a hero
        A hero… Yeah ok

I finally get the opportunity
To tell you what he did to me
You sympathize and you agree
You're just another employee

You go and knock upon the door
His past record you just ignore
You say, there's not much you can do
My mom was right, you're *just another man wearing blue*

"Excuse me sir, you've been accused of this, and this, and that"
"I'm innocent"
"I'm sorry to bother you"

And then you tip your hat.

While all along, I'm in the back and I can only pray
I'm right back here, come rescue me
Please sir, come save the day
And once again, like every time, you simply walk away

GOOD JOB!!!
    BRAVO!!!
        YOU STUPID PIG!!!

You sure helped me a bunch
I hope you choke on something
I'm sure you're on your way to lunch

Meanwhile I sit here drowning
In my bloody sorrow
Wondering if I'm even going to
Make it to tomorrow

For future reference
I'll recall, to handle it alone
And when I think to call for help
I won't pick up the phone

He thinks that since he got away scot-free
It means he won
I know one thing, he bet' not try
To come back for my son

He took away my sympathy
And taught me way too much
Like how to work a gun
And how not to give a "you know what"

Or maybe I'll get crazy
And I'll slice, and dice, and chop
And when they ask me why I did it
I'll blame it on the cop!

# BULLETPROOF

Some people get shot
And bleed out
Others become
Bulletproof

I'm no longer bound by his chains
Neither will I be bound by his remains
I've finally been set free
I finally get to be me

No longer a prisoner of the age 18
My shackles are broken
My slate wiped clean

Sure, people will continue to talk
They'll continue to call me a hoe
But people often talk the most
'Bout things that they don't know

You see, I've been to hell and back
From 18 to 19, that whole entire year
Each day was another adventure
Filled with misery, pain, and fear

Of course, I tried to run away
I even tried to hide
No matter where I hid, he found me
And gave me good reason to cry

I thought I could hide on campus
With security, dorms locked tight
I was sure this time I'd win
Little did I know, that the ones I called my friends
Would be the ones to let him in

I was trying to be a hero
Protect my family and all
I suppose, trying to handle things myself
Is what lead to my downfall

So finally, I went to authorities
Like I should've done at first
But damn, if they didn't help at all
They only made it worse

I knew what I had to do,
If I really wanted him to go
But there's so much to the story
Still so much that you don't know

I got down on my knees and prayed,
"Lord take this cup from me"
I'm finally ready to let go
I'm ready to be free

Within days, one problem solved
Another developing inside
But, this one gave me will to live
And strength enough to fight

My Birthday, what a perfect time
To have this weight lifted off my shoulder
No longer a prisoner of the age 18
I was now another year older

I've learned so many lessons
From one year to the next
I'm so much wiser now
I feel I've passed the test

So, gossip if you must
Spread rumors if you please
You cannot take this joy I have
My soul is now at ease

# A SUDDEN PAUSE IN MY SOUL

(gasping for air)
Oh … damn!
I forgot to breath
I was lost in the image
of the vision
he was verbally giving to me
that before, my mind
wouldn't have even
been able to conceive,
because of past experiences
that would never allow me to see
or believe

(staring in a daze)
Damn girl…
You gotta blink
I was blinded by his presence
I was trapped in a dream
and I couldn't help but stare
What's crazy is he wasn't even there
He was whispering wisdom
over miles of telephone
And his presence filled the air
I could feel him everywhere

(sigh… gasp… chuckle)
My heart just skipped a beat
I was overwhelmed by the notion
that he sees so much in me
And of how I make him feel
and the way I know it's real

There are things you can't explain, things you can't put into words
And my soul comes to a sudden stop
Because when he speaks, it's like he already knows

I'm doing time
    for someone else's crime
I'm paying the price
    for someone else's wrong lived life

I had to suffer, became a mother… the road I had to take
    for someone else' dumb mistake

I had a son… He's on the run… He got away
    Yet I'm the one who has to pay… Everyday.

When I was doing wrong, seemed things would go so right
    So now I'm called to suffer 'cause
        I choose to walk with Christ?

I asked God to use me, I guess this means, He has
    I know I'm doing good,
        when things are going so bad

My body is a temple, a living sacrifice
    And I know that my reward, is to have eternal life

Still, I can't help but question,
    why they don't have these trials

I chose to be a virgin;
    they chose to go run wild

"It's just not fair!", I cry
    "You said I'd reap what I sow!"

You answer me,
    "They weren't called to go where you will go!"

I've been a prisoner far too long,
    Although, my debt was fully paid

My suffering cannot compare,
      My cross, I would not trade

I vowed that I would die for him,
      I love my God so dearly

He asks, instead, I live for Him
      I live my life sincerely

A ransom so great, exchanged for me
      I'll never comprehend

I rest assured of recompense
      if I can reach the end

Although I know, happiness ain't real
I want it to last a while longer
I want to be happy during the trails
That come to make me stronger

I know he cannot love me
But he always says he does
And I want to feel this momentary
Felling of being loved

Sometimes I think people are so busy
    trying to figure out what I am,
    they can never really see who I am.

Why was I inflicted with this disease,
    whose name is secret?
    I am a **proud black woman**,
    but why can't they see it?

Will I be forced to live this way
    for the rest of my life?
    Striving to be accepted
    by those who are like me?

No one is like me.
    No one knows what it's like
    to be ethnically invisible.

People have some nerve telling me
    how beautiful I am,
    then turn around and say
    I'm conceited, because I know it.

Beauty is in the eye of the beholder;
    and I don't like what I behold.
    I don't like who I see in the mirror.

Self-esteem by definition, is confidence
    in one's own worth
    or abilities; self respect.

So, where do you get it?

One would argue that it comes from within,
    that's why it's called **self**-esteem,
    but I beg to differ.

It comes from what you are taught;
      what you are told.
      It comes from with-out.

If you've spent your entire life
      being asked what you are,
      you may find yourself
      questioning your identity as well.

When white says, you're too black
      and black says, you're too white,
      where does that leave you?
      Lost in the middle somewhere.

No one can see you;
      the color of your skin is invisible.
      No one can miss someone invisible,
         when they're gone.

# STARING DOWN THE BARREL OF A GUN

I stared down the barrel of a gun,
  but my life didn't flash before my eyes

Instead I filled with anger
  This may come as no surprise

  *"Go ahead! Shoot me so, I can beat yo ass!"*

I know it wouldn't have really happened that way
  but that's how I recall the moment
  as I look into the past

I couldn't even be afraid
My emotions were numb by then
I already wanted to die
I longed for the bullet at the other end

I looked fear dead in the eyes
Then I pushed my forehead against the tip

  *"Hold out your foot!", he said,
  trying to break my brave exterior.*

It worked.

But it didn't change what I like to remember.

  *"Wait... What?
  You've got to be out your mind if you think
  I'm just gonna let you blow my foot off.
  You'll be better off killing me!
  I will limp my one footed ass over there
  and beat the hell out of you with my good foot!"*

Looking back on my life's storms
  I can only make light of the situations

Terrible circumstances are often where
    comedians find their best inspiration

What good does it do me to dwell on the past?
By reliving the moments as they *really* were,
    I only make them last

While things like that you can't forget;
    it's better if you laugh

He only wins if I keep the fear in my heart
    that the gun was meant to instill
Instead I bear witness to where God as brought me
Despite it all, I'm still in His will

If I keep this fact in mind
I can joke and I can rhyme
Although my life was threatened
I will not stay a victim to this crime

And you know what?

It's almost like, that gun had just as much affect
    as a microphone in his hand

The gun that didn't kill me, only made me stronger.
And because I looked down into the abyss
I can choose not to suffer any longer

So don't cry for me, just learn from me
    and laugh with me too

        *",Cause if that mother…. Would have….*
        *Do you know?"*

But I refuse
I refuse to leave my soul standing there
staring down the barrel of a gun

There she is
    the woman with a
    breastplate of steel
Cooking, cleaning, fast as lightning
    'Because she knows
    if she doesn't do it
    then nobody will

Taking the pressure upon herself
Not wanting to put it on anyone else
Forgetting that she's had help all along
Probably 'cause she'd gotten so used
    to doing things on her own

With her superman now by her side,
    she keeps trying to carry him on her back
'cause she knows he works so hard and he
    should be able to come home
    and just relax

She makes sure she's done all of her chores
    tries to clear her mind of her stressful day
So that she can be attentive
    and be able to retain
    everything he has to say

Phenomenal woman,
    Yeah… that's she
With one child on her hip
    and the other on her knee

She smiles through her tears and her pain
'Cause she can't stand for her child
    to look at her that way
A blank stare of confusion as if to say

*"Mommy's superwoman how can she cry,*
*and if she's so weak, then what am I"*

She sings Itsy-Bitsy, and ABC's
She wants to buy them everything
But money don't grow on trees

But she keeps on keepin' on
Knowing they don't understand
And by her example, she raises her children
To be strong, righteous, Supermen

She puts her family first
Sometimes, she doesn't even eat
But it doesn't matter as long as they
Get a good night's sleep

Keeping everyone happy
        is what makes her so strong
Sometimes she forgets,
        we *all* need somebody to lean on

Catching a glimpse of herself in the mirror
        With dark circles under her eyes
At 21, she should be able to think much clearer
        And to her it comes as a surprise

That a bulletproof vest
        can only take so many shots
And she has to admit,
        she has taken a lot

She's constantly telling herself
        *"don't you cry, don't you break down"*

But it's hard to find something else to clean
And it's hard not to think,
        when there's no one around

Still, she keeps working while perfecting herself
Learning from every mistake
Gaining wisdom, and courage
Reminding herself, that there's no task too great

*"Hey, what's that up in the sky?"*

It's a bird.

It's a plane.

No, it's superwoman

and she's ready to fly.

Dissolution

    Closure

        Termination

            Ending

                Suspension

                    Conclusion

I didn't sign on for that!

We were married, when I made a vow
    to share my life with him.
To share his problems, to share his pain,
    to share in good times

You know, "sunshine and rain".

And it ain't take no papers, to make it that way.

I was fooled and was astounded to discover
    that the man I married, had become another.

I've had guns to my face, and have shown no fear
    why is it I can't hide the pain, when he comes near.

For he's angry, and he's distant, and I cannot help;
    but I didn't marry him to let him go
    through this by himself.

What's the confusion, perhaps a misunderstanding?
What am I doing wrong?

Or maybe it's just, I was blinded by love,
    but that man's been there all along.

I'm so sorry God
      for the mistake I've made
      but now I need your help out!

Carry me through this
      or make it better
Whatever you do, let me have no doubt.

Confirmation came on that day,
      the lunchbox hit me in my mouth.

We were divorced, when I knew
      I'd tried all I could
      to reconcile and understand.

Even when I was made to feel worthless and afraid.
Chance after chance I gave.
Passionate and loving I stayed.
My hope in him, was the only thing that changed.
I will never make that same mistake.

I made a vow to God, and not to man,
      but now, I have to take that vow back again.

And it ain't take no papers, to make it that way.

I should've known by the way that he kissed
        that it was wrong
That I should just leave it alone
That something like this can't go on

There's more static in a forbidden kiss.

I should've known by the way the fire burned inside
        and the electricity sparked
With the kiss of his lips and the touch of his hands
That that's where it should end
        and we should just be friends

Forbidden fruit is often sweetest.

But there's no denying I wanted him more
Watching him stretch and workout didn't help
And although I was aware of his mad love affair
        I wanted him all to myself

The gleam in his eyes, had me hypnotized
Every curve of his body, and them thick sexy lips
Had me craving him like strawberries and cool whip
        or some chips and some cheddar cheese dip

No words can express
        the feelings I felt
With his body on top of mine
I'd give anything just to be able
To pause that one moment in time

When our skins collide
With our legs entwined,
        and his body inside of mine

I saw the stars that night
I saw them in his eyes
At that moment he lost focus
    of the one he'd been thinking of all this time

At that moment I was happy
At that moment I was in love
At that moment my heart was
    singing a joyous song

Now I must say goodbye
Trying hard not to cry
It just goes to show you
Happiness don't last long

I'll choose to recall,
for the sake of writing this
The time I was betrayed
by true love's violent kiss

I saw the signs ahead of time,
so really can't complain
He always had an anger streak,
But he called *me* insane

He'd say I shouldn't dress like that
Judgmental, yet deceiving
He lost it when he saw I'd packed
He knew that I was leaving

I felt his hands around my throat
He held me in the air
I quickly sorted through my options
As my body dangled there

I could fight back, of course
I had a weapon in my pocket
Perfectly positioned to kick him in the groin
Then I'd stab and wouldn't stop it

But I didn't want him to die
My love was forever, 'cause it's real
But he must have hated me
His actions showed, how he must feel

Option two, I disappear
        or elevate, so to speak
Choosing not to need much air
I've trained throughout my childhood
to take myself away from here

If I didn't do it quick,
      I'd probably go unconscious
So, I floated up above myself
Observing what was taking place
Knowing I couldn't call for help
And knowing, I couldn't stop it

He probably thought I'd died
So, after what seemed way too long
He threw me in the closet

I heard him walk away, as I returned to my flesh
So in shock and heartbroken
That I couldn't feel the pain
And it's strange, I felt sorrier for him, than myself

When he was gone, and I knew the coast was clear
More decisions had to be made

Should I call for help?
Would he return?
Maybe he's sorry…

He called my phone just moments later
      to tell me that he was
But by then, it was too late,
      the authorities were on the way
And I regret that phone call till this day

I told myself before, to never trust a cop again
This justice system's so screwed up
Even when I tried to drop the charges
They spent years reminding me,
      this system's not my friend

Dragged through court,
unsure if he deserved it
Knowing that I didn't,
but I called them, so I earned it

They shared with me his record,
       prior to my arrival
They wouldn't let him be
       Not without penalty
I hate that it had to be me
But his sentence may mean,
       his next victim's survival

And although it seemed he'd changed
And my heart was still entangled
I could never return,
       'cause I could never forget
The day my love was strangled

Wrote down a verse
No need to rehearse
I know what it's like
I've been in this fight

I hustled real hard
Had to give it to God
I gave up the bad
To get what he had

I was embarrassed
And I was ashamed
I needed an out
And someone to blame

Ain't tryna be greedy
Ain't tryna get rich
Just provide so my family
Won't live in a ditch

You see I was homeless
And lost everything
So, I know what it's like
To be desperate in chains

Feeling worthless, in bondage
Determined to change
Generational curses
I break every chain

Like you I justified it
Where is the sin
Who am I hurting?
Again, and again
I suffered within
Passed down to my kin

I've spent all my life trying
to break generational curses
of poverty, sickness and death

Didn't like who I saw in the mirror,
the role that I played
I wouldn't wish it on nobody else

Identity faded, but I was created
       for a greater purpose
They ask, "who she think she is?"

I'm not better than ya'll,
       but I'm better than this.

Sorry if my testimony
hit a sore spot for you
But somebody's asking,
"Lord what must I do"

I did it for the money
Some just do it for attention
And people may judge me
for telling my business

But many relate;
       Can I get a witness?

Let them without sin, cast the first stone
Tryna let you know, you're not alone
To God be the Glory, for He rescued me
The person I was, I will no longer be

# ARRAIGNED

When you believe in
Guilty until proven innocent
Things don't hurt as bad

Expecting the worst
Hoping for the best

If found innocent
Be overjoyed
You didn't expect it

If guilty is the verdict
Well
It's no surprise

She stands, bare breasted
in front of the mirror,
heart still pounding through her chest
trying to slowly remove each sticky nuisance
from the machine that monitored her vitals
just moments ago

She stands there, staring at her reflection
Eyes almost literally turning black
She imagines her heart is doing the same

She never wanted it to end this way
She'd hoped that her life
would have been worth more

If we all must die, she wanted to
have laid down her life
for the love of someone else
She wanted to be a sacrifice

Now it is love that takes her life in vain
She reflects on all the good
she would have accomplished
had she not been broken

Now destruction she will bring
until her heart gives out
One can only take so much pain
shouldn't be long now

She prays she'll leave this shell
        before too much damage is done
There's still good somewhere in her
She always knew what she was capable of
She never wanted to become this darkness
        but they smothered out her light.

*"But the time is coming—indeed it's here now—when you will be scattered, each one going his own way, leaving me alone. Yet I am not alone because the Father is with me." (John 16:32)*

Alone.
Surrounded by people,
      but it's all I've ever been.

You of all people know, it's the saddest place to be.
Especially when you're alone in your own home.
When you were unloved from the womb it's hard to escape.
You become an adult who will marry
      and have kids and live in a house full of alone.

No one to understand you.

No one to talk to.

All you have is God.
You'll feel guilty telling yourself,
HE alone should be enough.

But even the Bible says…

*"Then the Lord God said, 'It is not good for the man to be alone. I will make a helper who is just right for him.'" (Genesis 2:18)*

You realize, this is not what He wanted for you.
It's not good.
When will someone see you in this crowd?
When will you be found in this darkness?
How long must you live alone?

*"Let your unfailing love surround us, Lord, for our hope is in you alone." (Psalms 33:22)*

# THE UGLY WALLS

Once upon a time, there was a woman who owned a home whose walls were not very pleasing to the eye. Once, the walls had been beautiful, but over time they had become worn and were starting to deteriorate. Now they were cracked, and battered, and the color had faded.

When guests would visit, they would point out the walls saying, "These walls are hideous and should be torn down".

But the woman loved her walls and knew that there must be something she could do to make them better. So, she added a fresh coat of paint, and hung up pictures, and plaques. She installed shelving so that she could display all the trophies she had ever won.

The woman was very pleased with the results, and although she remembered how the walls looked before, she was so proud of the hard work she had put into her walls, to make them good as new.

She invited her neighbors over to view her new walls, but when they got there, they did not admire the lovely trophies or the new coat of paint. In fact, instead of congratulating her on her accomplishment, they continued to ridicule and insult the walls as if they had never changed at all.

Some of them said, "Is that a hole I see?"

Others said, "Why is there no border around these walls?"

Some even said that the walls were so ugly before the transformation, they couldn't even focus on what they looked like now. They couldn't help but recall, what the walls used to be.

And the woman was sad, because no one had noticed the beauty in her walls, and all she had gone through to get them that way.

I look at him and smile
With my eyes
With my whole face
He makes me smile
 with my whole being

My smile fades as the fear creeps in
Not because of anything he's done wrong
But because I recall
 the last time I was here
The last time I took this fall

He makes me hope for a brighter future
The one I used to dream of
My happily ever after
The one I'd come to believe was just
 A fairy tale; unheard of

He's the unrealistic expectation
 I'd prayed for
A figment of my imagination
But he's real, and he's here, and he's mine
 Am I dreaming, have I died?

He is heaven on earth
He brings me peace

When I'm with him
I know my worth
No longer worthless,
 yet still so hurt

I wish I could erase
 the bad memories of love
The ones that fade with passing time

He tells me, he loves me, often
But I've learned not to believe in words
   Especially those.

His actions speak as he adores me
And I'm afraid because I don't want to fail him
   as I did them
My heart still breaks for loves lost
My guilt still eats away at me because
I was told everything was all my fault

Maybe it was,
   maybe I shouldn't have loved
   so quickly, so hard, so endlessly

If only I could stop caring,
   as they have so easily done
I could fly away with my love
In blissful happiness without a care
Without a fear that one day,
   he too will change

I was so willing to jump to my death
With the painful love that was inflicted upon me
Yet here I stand so hesitant to jump
Into something that could change my life
   Something that could really be

So, I'm tiptoeing slowly down this cliff
Only to realize that the closer I get to him
   the more alive I feel
I haven't written a poem in years
I feel awake and I know it's him

The reason.

He's waking up something in me.
You can call it a Queen, or call it a Beast
It's powerful, and I'm open

In places I had put up walls
      for my own protection
Not wanting my children to experience
Yet another man's rejection

All the "what ifs" taking over because
If not for the "should haves"
I could have avoided all this pain
So maybe now I better not

I know better.

Or maybe I can close the door
      on those chapters that grew me to this point.

Maybe this can be the beginning of a reaping
      I've sown for so long.

I can't get back all those years
All those tears
All that wasted time
So now I make every second count
I wish I could go back and speak
For a moment
To who she used to be
I'd give her some advice
I'd warn her of the coming trails
I'd hug her tight
Maybe I'd have avoided so much pain
Maybe she wouldn't be who she is today

# I AM

I AM afraid
I AM unsure
I often worry, panic, and complain
I AM completely justified in that, at times

I AM a mother
I AM a wife
I AM a daughter
I AM a sister
I AM a public figure
I have responsibilities in life;
       people depend on me, to do what's right

I AM expected to do great things
       because I AM has called my name

I AM courageous
I AM strong
I AM's been with me all along

I AM determined
       but I AM tired

I AM leaning on the one who sent me
I AM trusting in His will

I AM judged
I AM criticized
I AM burdened beyond comprehension
I AM understands;
      He's been there
I have no more excuses

I AM sent me
      I have to go

I AM winning,
      I have won

And soon
      I AM will say, *"Well done!"*

## SUICIDE

If you or someone you know is struggling with depression, please seek help immediately. You don't have to struggle alone! Sometimes you have to reach out to someone who can help carry you when you can't carry yourself. I also encourage you to get a prayer partner for those times when you can't even pray for yourself.

# National Suicide Prevention Lifeline
1-800-273-8255

**How do I know they are suicidal?**
Here are a few ways to recognize when someone may be suicidal... From someone who has been there many times, I can tell you, I exhibited ALL of these at some point. No one ever noticed or attempted to stop me. It made the feeling that much harder to resist. Therefore, I am a firm believer that suicide **CAN** be prevented, if you know what you're dealing with.

- **Excessive sadness or moodiness**
- **Hopelessness**
- **Increased use of drugs or alcohol**
- **Trouble Sleeping, or Excessive sleeping**
- **Sudden calmness** after a period of depression.
- **Withdrawal** from friends and/or family. They'd rather be alone.
- **Changes in personality and/or appearance** – they'll often stop taking care of their hygiene during this time, finding it difficult to take showers or care what they look like.
- **Dangerous or self-harmful behavior –** when you don't care anymore, what have you got to lose?
- **Recent trauma or life crisis**

- **Making preparations** – like preparing a will, getting their affairs in order, planning how they may kill themselves, like purchasing a gun for example. Also, they may write a note to leave behind or want to tell their loved ones goodbye in some other way.
- **Threatening suicide** - Not everyone considering suicide will speak up, but often times, we want someone to know and help us before we do something we'll regret. We may mention it in passing and if it's ignored, assume that no one cares.

### What should I do if I see these signs?

If you believe someone you know is in immediate danger of harming or killing himself or herself:

- **Do not leave the person alone.** Even if you are just present to allow them to cry on your shoulder, being alone with their own thoughts is the last place they should be.
- **Confiscate weapons.** You may have to literally remove anything the person could use to hurt himself or herself. You may even have to think outside the box. If a person is desperate enough, they can think of a lot of ways to hurt themselves. If you can't remove all the dangerous items, take them somewhere safe. I literally used to go into my water closet, where there is nothing but a toilet. I couldn't possibly figure out how to kill myself with one of those.
- **Contact a doctor or therapist**. You may be able to suggest or help him or her contact the doctor or therapist for guidance and help. The suicide hotline is also a very helpful resource.
- **Keep them calm.** Sometimes it's just a matter of waiting for the current emotion to pass. If you can be there to talk them through what they are feeling, listen, and not judge, this could mean life or death for many people! Be careful not to give too much advice though, or insist, "it isn't that bad." Trust me, whatever they are dealing with at that moment, they probably feel like, no matter what you may have been through, you can't possibly understand.

- **Call 911 or take the person to an emergency room**. If it is serious enough that they are cutting themselves, have taken some pills or any other harmful action, you may have to call for emergency help right away. Just be there with them as they go through this process.

I hope this information helps. There are several people that come to mind in my own past that I would have loved to drill this information into. Unfortunately, some people will never understand. Know that God does, and keep reminding yourself that He would never put more on you than you can bear.

## ABUSE

Children are being abused around the world every single day. Some may never reach adulthood. Others can be saved. It's up to each of us to pay attention to the signs. If you suspect someone of child abuse, get involved. Call for help and assistance. It takes a village.

# Child Abuse Hotline
1-800-4-A-CHILD (2-24453)

Children aren't the only ones experiencing abuse. Often, if you've been abused as a child, you'll attract the same as an adult. It's an unfortunate generational curse. And abuse is **not** just physical. Love should NEVER hurt. If you are in a relationship that has become physically or mentally abusive, GET OUT NOW! Don't allow yourself to be the next victim on the news. And don't be too naïve, to think that it can't happen to you. It's best to never find out!

# Domestic Violence Hotline
1-800-799-SAFE (7233)

# DEALING WITH THE NARCISSIST

There are many situations and emotions I have experienced throughout life, that may have been avoided, had I had a better understanding of narcissists—who they are and how they operate. As an adult, and after several years of counseling and group therapy, I can now say that I do. Because of my studies of the Holy Bible, it is also clear to me, as I referenced in the beginning of this book, that narcissism is one of those many evil spirits we must be able to stand against. Due to our lack of knowledge, it is destroying families every day.

Thanks to the knowledge I've gained, I can let go of a lot of pain caused by consistently drawing this toxic personality into my life, whether that was a family member, friend or lover. It is a pattern that can, and must, be broken. I believe it starts with education.

It's important to remember that MILLIONS of people have this type of personality and MILLIONS of us deal with them every day. It is not your fault, nor is it your responsibility to "fix" them, as we so often want to do. Just pray for them, stay in your happy place, and keep it moving!

You can always Google more information—there's a lot of it out there. I recommend the article below by *HelpGuide.org*. It is very detailed and elaborates on some of the points I'll touch on.

**REFERENCE:**
https://www.helpguide.org/articles/mental-disorders/narcissistic-personality-disorder.htm

**(Authors: Melinda Smith, M.A. and Lawrence Robinson. Updated: December 2019.)**

# What is narcissistic personality disorder (NPD)?

According to Wikipedia…

*"**Narcissistic personality disorder (NPD)** is a personality disorder characterized by a long-term pattern of exaggerated feelings of self-importance, an excessive need for admiration, and a lack of empathy toward other people.[2][3] People with NPD often spend much time thinking about achieving power and success, or on their appearance.[3] Typically, they also take advantage of the people around them.[3] Such narcissistic behavior typically begins by early adulthood, and occurs across a broad range of situations.[3]*

*The causes of narcissistic personality disorder are unknown.[4] The condition of NPD is included in the cluster B personality disorders in the Diagnostic and Statistical Manual of Mental Disorders (DSM).[3] A diagnosis of NPD is made by a healthcare professional interviewing the person in question.[2] The condition of NPD should be differentiated from mania and substance use disorder.[3]*

*Treatments for narcissistic personality disorder have not been well studied.[2] Therapy is difficult, because people with narcissistic personality disorder usually do not consider themselves to have a mental health problem.[2] About one percent of people are believed to be affected with NPD at some point in their lives.[4] It occurs more often in men than women, and typically affects younger as opposed to older people.[2][3] The narcissistic personality was first described by the psychoanalyst Robert Waelder, in 1925; and the term narcissistic personality disorder (NPD) was coined by Heinz Kohut, in 1968.[5][6]"*

## What are the signs and symptoms?

- Grandiose sense of self-importance
- Lives in a fantasy world that supports their delusions
- Needs constant praise and admiration
- Sense of entitlement
- Exploits others without guilt or shame
- Frequently demeans, intimidates, bullies, or belittles others
- Charming & Convincing - Don't fall for it!

Does this sound like anyone you know?

## How do I protect myself?

The answer to this can vary depending on *who* you are dealing with. In some cases, it's a parent; other times, it's a spouse or friend. You are the only one who can determine the value of your relationship and how to deal with this particular person. I will warn you, however, be careful that you are dealing with them and protecting your own safety and health in the process. Remember that if you continue to allow the abuse they inflict, you'll likely continue to draw it from others, causing generational curses to ensue. It's important to think about your future, and the future of your future.

- **Set healthy boundaries** – You deserve respect as much as anyone. So, demand it. Don't allow anyone to disrespect or trample on you. It's up to you to draw the line.

- **Don't take things personally** – They will try to convince you that their behavior is somehow your fault. It's not! They are narcissists and you didn't do anything to make them that way!

- **Don't argue with them** – It's impossible and since they are always right—in their own mind—they will always win. You'll stress yourself out arguing in a battle that can't be won. Walk away knowing you are right—if you are of course.

- **Look for support and purpose elsewhere** – These people are great at isolating you. Make sure you are following your dreams, have your own friends, social life, confide in others. If you don't, he/she can easily make you believe in their reality simply because you don't know any other. You'll believe the way they treat you is normal, because you won't have a good reference, if you aren't around normal people who treat each other kindly.

- **Get out!** - In many cases, the only option is to run for your life. There's nothing wrong with trying, but whatever their behavior is now, will usually only escalate if you let it. At a certain point, it may be time to let them go before it gets any worse. You may have to seek professional help, move out of state, and cut all contact. Again, the options will vary depending on the situation.

# HOW TO HEAL?

Regardless of what type of abuse, neglect, or emotional trauma you have experienced, it's important to know that there are options. You are not alone. You aren't the first person to experience this, and you won't be the last. My book alone should tell you that much.

If you recognize the problem, at some point, it is time to focus on the solution. Remember that these moments will pass. They are only moments in your years of life. If you are still alive, you still have a purpose. Find out what that is and focus on it. Don't let it get too late.

Allow yourself to grieve. What you've gone through is painful. This is the reality. Crying is healthy. Find ways to vent so that you don't explode. Some healthy ways of expressing these feelings are: exercise, writing, journaling, spending time in nature, singing, dancing, or participating in a sport or activity you enjoy.

This can be easier said than done, so it helps to have an accountability partner for the times when you can't bring yourself to cope. Make sure someone knows what you are going through: a pastor, friend, family member or counselor. Even when we feel like we are all alone, there is always someone else. If not, make sure you get out and socialize during the times you're able to so you can expand your circle. Just don't deal with it alone.

Sometimes, you may have to be a little selfish. If it's all just too much, take a spa day. Cut your phone off and shut out the world just to focus on **you** for a change. I personally started waking up at 4am every morning to have what I call "me and God time," then I hit the gym. It is the only way I'm able to start my day off on a positive note, before my kids and husband wake up, before the phone starts ringing, and before duty calls. For a few hours, I am able to do what I want, without interruption, and it has changed how I handle the daily tasks ahead.

Don't expect so much from people. Everyone has their reasons for what they do. We are all human. We all have emotions and react to things that take place in our lives in our own way. We all were raised by someone who may not have gotten it all right all the time, so we carry that into our adult behavior. As much as you allow yourself to be human, don't expect any different from others. Create boundaries on how you allow people to treat you. Then, if or when they disappoint you, don't blame yourself. Just allow them to be them...sometimes that means away from you. Sometimes you have to block their number; unfriend them on social media. There is nothing wrong with that. Just make sure you aren't silently suffering due to someone else's actions, while they probably sleep pretty good at night.

You decide how you react, and how you feel. Take control. Ask God for help. Especially with those things that are so heavy, you know that you can't carry on your own. It's not weakness, it's faith!

On that note, I'll leave off with one of my favorite poems, whose author is unknown... It's reminder has gotten me through a lot of hardships.

### FOOTPRINTS IN THE SAND

*One night I dreamed a dream.*
*As I was walking along the beach with my Lord.*
*Across the dark sky flashed scenes from my life.*
*For each scene, I noticed two sets of footprints in the sand,*
*One belonging to me and one to my Lord.*

*After the last scene of my life flashed before me,*
*I looked back at the footprints in the sand.*
*I noticed that at many times along the path of my life,*

*especially at the very lowest and saddest times,*
*there was only one set of footprints.*

*This really troubled me, so I asked the Lord about it.*
*"Lord, you said once I decided to follow you,*
*You'd walk with me all the way.*
*But I noticed that during the saddest and most troublesome times of my life,*
*there was only one set of footprints.*
*I don't understand why, when I needed You the most, You would leave me."*

*He whispered, "My precious child, I love you and will never leave you*
*Never, ever, during your trials and testings.*
*When you saw only one set of footprints,*
*It was then that I carried you."*

# THANK YOU             TO READERS

Thank you for purchasing my book and helping me share my story! I appreciate your support and hope you will continue to follow me on this journey.  As I mentioned before, this is just the beginning.  I have several stage productions, movies, and books that will soon follow and give more insight to my life and my purpose.

I invite you to **subscribe to my website** and follow me on social media, to keep track of details as they develop.

Thank you again for your support!


## Vitelle.net

# ABOUT THE AUTHOR

A native of Dayton, Ohio, Vitelle has always been gifted with a multitude of talents. Starting out in school plays, from elementary to college, she was a natural performer; although her opportunities were limited as a child. Despite many setbacks in life, she continued to walk in her calling. Even as a young mother and wife, she balanced life's responsibilities and expectations, while still pursuing a career in film and television. By her early 20's, she had made a name for herself in Kentucky and surrounding states. In 2009, she decided to relocate her family to Atlanta, Georgia to pursue her dreams further.

Since then, Vitelle has traveled nationwide performing in a multitude of films, music videos, commercials, fashion shows, and stage productions. As if this wasn't enough, she also wears the hat of a public speaker, writer, and director. With a passion in community activism, she uses her career in entertainment as a platform to help people in need across the globe.

As a mother of three, Vitelle juggles a family and her entertainment career all while helping others to achieve their goals. In 2010, she officially founded her first non-profit organization called, "The Feed the Homeless Tour", despite the fact that her own family was homeless at that time.

With roles in films & TV shows such as TYLER PERRY'S "I CAN DO BAD ALL BY MYSELF", LIFETIME'S "DROP DEAD DIVA", & The CW's "VAMPIRE DIARIES", Vitelle took a step back from the spotlight to focus on her stage production, "THE FACE OF HOMELESS", which premiered in Atlanta, GA in August 2013; and for the first time tied both her career and passion for helping the homeless together into one beautiful package. The show depicts Vitelle's real life testimony of the struggle raising a family, balancing several jobs, and still helping others in need, while living homeless in their car. It is the first of many true stories to be told.

By her early 30's, Vitelle had experienced divorce, depression, human trafficking, narcissistic abuse, domestic violence, suicide attempts, homelessness, being a single mom, and countless other struggles, which she has journaled and documented throughout her life in hopes to one day be a living testimony. She believes that all of the struggles meant for her destruction, can be used to change the world by sharing her experiences through the arts. This rising star is the true definition of determination as she continues to rise to the top no matter what circumstances life may bring.

Made in the USA
Columbia, SC
31 January 2025

52575475R00059